SCOTTISH CLANS

by
ALAN BOL

KT-433-319

The clan system received its death-blow, with
the clansmen, at the Battle of Culloden in 1746,
when clans loyal to the Stuarts were mercilessly
punished by order of the Duke of Cumberland,
highland dress was proscribed, the clans were
disarmed, and even the bagpipes were banned
as an instrument of war. To understand how
the clansman was resuscitated to become a
national folk-hero and the mainstay of the
tourist industry, it is necessary to follow his
rise and fall into posthumous grace.

Post-Roman Alba was divided among four groups, three of whom – the Picts, the Scots and the Britons – were of Celtic origin. The fourth group, the Angles, who settled in the Lothians, were part of that savage 5th-century Teutonic invasion of Britain that scattered the native Britons into Strathclyde, Wales and Cornwall. As far as Alba was concerned, the immediate future was to be in the hands of the Picts and Scots.

The Scots came to Alba from Antrim in Northern Ireland to establish a colony in and around Argyllshire. They called their colony Dalriada after their mother country in Antrim and adapted so well to the new environment that they eventually preferred it to the original Dalriada. In c.500 Fergus Mor, son of Erc, set up a new dynasty in Dalriada and established a capital at Dunadd. With this permanent foothold in Alba the ambitious Scots began to take steps to extend their influence. To begin with, Fergus and his brothers divided Dalriada amongst themselves, thus forming the first district clans: Cinel Lorn, Cinel Garran, Cinel Comgall and Cinel Angus.

It was an Irish Scot who brought a dynasty and territorial ambition to Alba and another Irish Scot, Columba, who brought Christianity (though St Ninian had, admittedly, made some inroads). When Columba came to Alba in 563 the Picts controlled most of the country north of the Forth. From his small monastery on the tiny island of Iona, off the west coast of Mull, Columba began to spread Christianity throughout the country. From Dalriada he went up the Great Glen and gradually persuaded the pagan Picts to renounce their Druidic beliefs and embrace Christianity. Columba's great theological victory was the first stage in the Scottish cultural conquest of Pictland.

At the end of the 8th century the Norsemen began to attack the Northern coast and islands of Alba. Not only did they permanently transform the character of the Hebrides, the Orkneys and the Shetlands, but the sustained pressure of the Norse raids on the mainland exhausted the Picts. In 843, when Kenneth MacAlpin, the king of the Dalriadic Scots, had established a controversial claim to the Pictish throne, he was able to win the argument convincingly. As king of the Scots and kinsman of the Picts he had himself crowned king of both at the Pictish sacred centre of Scone.

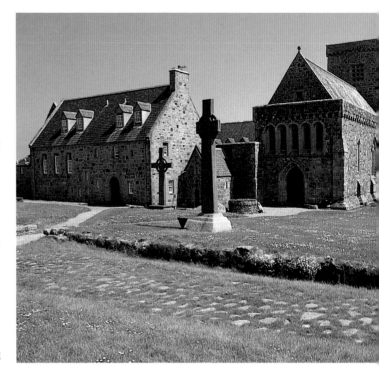

This union of the Picts and the Scots under the Dalriadic king meant the end of Pictland and the beginning of the dominance of the Gaelic-speaking Scots. It was not, because of the work of Columba, a sudden event. Yet now the Picts had a religion, a culture and a king imposed on them and in time they were absorbed completely by the Scots.

In 1018 the Celtic king, Malcolm II, brought the Lothians under Scottish rule and in 1034 Malcolm II's grandson, Duncan, became king of a geographically united Scotland. The Celts were not to control the kingdom. In 1040 Duncan was killed in battle (not, despite Shakespeare, in bed) by Macbeth, who was killed in turn by Duncan's son, Malcolm, in 1058. Malcolm III, or Malcolm Canmore (from the Gaelic Ceann-Mor meaning 'great chief') is credited with alienating the Gaels and initiating that Scottish antagonism between clans and crown.

Because of his English upbringing, Malcolm preferred the Anglo-Saxon Lothians to the Celtic north. In 1066 he had himself crowned at Dunfermline rather than Scone. Rather more dramatically, that year saw the Normans conquer England and an influx of Saxon refugees into the Lothians. Malcolm welcomed them with open arms and even

Above, top: Iona Abbey and St Martin's Cross. On this tiny island of Iona, off Mull, Columba founded a monastery in AD 563. It became a centre of Celtic Christianity and Columba's base.

Above: David I and his grandson Malcolm IV. David introduced Norman methods of government and became the most powerful 12th-century Scottish king. A pale shadow of his grandfather, Malcolm's appearance earned him the nickname 'the Maiden'

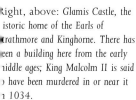

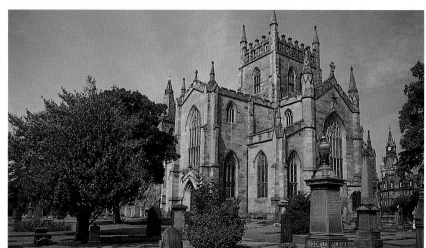

Right, above: *Glamis Castle, the historic home of the Earls of Strathmore and Kinghorne. There has been a building here from the early middle ages; King Malcolm II is said to have been murdered in or near it in 1034.*

Right, centre: *Dunfermline Abbey, Fife. Since Malcolm Canmore's time this 12th-century Benedictine abbey replaced Iona as the sepulchre of the Scottish kings.*

Right, below: *A detail of the Aberlemno Cross Slab showing Pictish warriors. The Picts were a Celtic race who, at the coming of the Dalriadic Scots to Alba (land of the Scots) from Dalriada (land of the Irish), controlled the entire east of the country, north of the Forth. They were converted to Christianity by Columba. Later, weakened by persistent Viking raids, they were pacified by Kenneth MacAlpin, king of the Dalriadic Scots, and united with the Scots in AD 853. Thereafter they were completely absorbed by the Scots and virtually disappear from history.*

married one of them: the Princess Margaret, sister of Edgar the Atheling. She was beautiful, fanatically religious, and a much more powerful personality than her illiterate husband. Under her influence Malcolm substituted Saxon for Gaelic as the court language, tried to force Roman Catholic rituals (like celibacy and poverty) on the Celtic clergy, and introduced feudalism into Celtic Scotland.

In principle, feudalism is the antithesis of the clan system. Under the clan ideal the land was held communally and administered by the chief. Under feudalism

Campbell • Cameron • Robertson
Mackay • MacDonald • Maclean
MacLeod • Mackinnon • MacDougall
Bruce

all land was royal land. The loyalty of the clansmen was that of kinsmen to their chief, not subjects to their king. The determination of successive kings to replace clannishness by feudalism drove a wedge between the Celtic Highlands and the Saxon Lowlands that continued up to Culloden.

Given the geography of the Scottish Highlands, it is not surprising that the Scottish kings found it difficult to assert their authority over people who lived among remote and inaccessible mountains. North of the Highland Line (that imaginary frontier stretching diagonally from the Clyde to the Tay) the clans associated themselves with well-defined natural areas that they claimed as family property. Deep glens surrounded by mountains and secure mainland areas became inhabited by clans: the Campbells in mid-Argyll, the Camerons in Lochaber, the Robertsons in Rannoch, the Mackays in Sutherland. Islands, too, attracted the great families: the MacDonalds in Islay, the Macleans in Mull, Tiree and Coll – while Skye was shared by MacDonalds, MacLeods and Mackinnons.

Despite the poverty of the soil, the clans attempted to be self-sufficient units living on the small cattle that somehow managed to survive the mountains. In the islands and on the coast the clansmen caught fish and exported their surplus to the Lowlands. In the glens they had barley for

fermenting whisky (mainly for the edification of the chief and gentlemen) and oats for making bread. It was a harsh way of life for the clansmen and, because cattle had to be protected, these Celtic hillsmen developed endurance and great military skill. In time their impetuosity in battle would startle Lowlander and Englishman alike.

The first clear personality to emerge in the story of the clans is Somerled, progenitor of Clan Donald, and the main figure in resisting the Norwegians, who controlled the Western Isles as well as Orkney and Shetland. Somerled was an outstanding warrior of mixed Pictish and Norse blood who, after a ferocious sea battle in 1156, gained the Kingship of Man, a Norwegian colony, which put him in control of all the Western Isles from

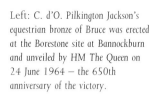

Left: C. d'O. Pilkington Jackson's equestrian bronze of Bruce was erected at the Borestone site at Bannockburn and unveiled by HM The Queen on 24 June 1964 – the 650th anniversary of the victory.

Right: A re-enactment of the Battle of Bannockburn.

Below, left: St Andrews Castle, Fife was originally built c.1200 by Bishop Roger and subsequently served as episcopal palace, fortress and state prison. After Bannockburn (1314) it was occupied and restored by Bishop William Lamberton, a staunch patriot and supporter of Bruce.

Below: Duntulm Castle in the Isle of Skye was a stronghold of the MacDonalds of Sleat.

Bute to Ardnamurchan Point. In return for a promise of fidelity Malcolm IV recognized Somerled's conquests. The difference was this: whereas Malcolm thought of Somerled holding his lands directly from the crown, Somerled regarded himself as an autonomous ruler, the King of the Isles.

In 1164, to show his defiance of the crown, Somerled sailed up the Clyde with 150 ships and sacked Glasgow. At Renfrew, however, he encountered the Steward of Scotland's army and was killed. Through his politically advantageous marriage to Ragnhildis, daughter of the Norwegian King of the Isles and Man, Somerled left three children, two of whom continued his line: Dougall founded the MacDougalls of Argyll and Lorn; and Reginald (whose son's name was Donald) the MacDonalds of Islay. In his own assertions of independence before the crown Somerled had set a precedent that would be emulated by his MacDonald descendants, the Lords of the Isles.

Not that many of the clans acted in concert. Even after the Norse occupation ended in 1266 Scotland was a land where clan fought against clan and the crown despaired of securing their loyalty. For example, although MacDougall of Lorn and

MacDonald of Islay opposed Bruce, the Clan Donald followed their chief's brother, Angus Og, and fought on Bruce's right at the Battle of Bannockburn. This gesture of allegiance strengthened the position of the MacDonalds and saved the disloyal members of the clan from punitive retaliation by Bruce. (After Bannockburn, the MacDonalds always claimed their place on the right in battle, a tradition disastrously ignored by Lord George Murray at Culloden.)

Divisions within clan groupings were, in fact, the rule rather than the exception as was demonstrated, painfully for those concerned, at the Battle of Inverhavon in 1370. The Camerons held land in Lochaber which the Mackintosh claimed was his. Not only did he continually reiterate his claim, but he took cattle from the Camerons as rent. After a particularly vindictive cattle raid by the Mackintosh the Camerons rallied 400 clansmen and marched into Badenoch, the territory of Clan Chattan. This confederation of clans included the Mackintoshes, the Davidsons, the Macphersons, the MacGillivrays, the MacBeans and the Farquharsons so, theoretically, it should have been possible for the combined forces of Clan Chattan to defeat the Camerons.

Certainly this was the Mackintosh's intention when, as Captain of Clan Chattan, he sent the *cran-taraidh* (fiery cross) around Badenoch and gathered the Macphersons and the Davidsons to his cause. Both clans claimed the place of honour on the Mackintosh's right and the argument was still raging when the Camerons arrived to do battle. Forced to make an instant decision, the Mackintosh gave the Davidsons the place on the right and, appalled at this, the Macphersons withdrew from the whole affair. They crossed the Spey and sat down to watch the combat. With a furious charge the Camerons cut the Davidsons to pieces and were in the act of finishing off the Mackintoshes when, at last, the Macphersons consented to join in and soon put the Camerons to flight.

Meanwhile, as the Clan Donald fell, the Clan Campbell rose (they take their name from the Gaelic *Cam-beul* meaning 'crooked mouth'). James IV, hammering home legalistic and feudal concepts, confirmed

many of the chiefs in their lands by royal parchment deed – 'sheepskin grants' – emphasizing that the vassal clans held their properties directly from the crown. James also gave Campbell of Argyll a three-year lease to several properties formerly held by the Lords of the Isles. With a strong base established in Argyllshire, the Campbells judiciously gave their support to whoever would give them most in return. They also set about completely dominating the land adjacent to them.

Being territorially acquisitive, the Campbells used any means to extend their influence throughout Argyllshire. The fate of the MacGregors illustrates this point. Because they held their land in Argyllshire and Perthshire on the clan principle, the MacGregors had no documentary evidence of ownership. They could appeal to

Above, left: Toward Castle, Argyll, stronghold of the Lamont Chiefs from the 15th century until it was destroyed by the Campbells in 1646.

Alastair Macdonell of Glengarry
(1771–1828)
This detail from a portrait by Raeburn shows a rather ostentatious figure. The high-necked tunic, the ivory-handled dirk, the decorative sporran all indicate that the costume is formal rather than functional. Colonel Macdonell is sometimes held to be the original of Fergus Mac-Ivor in *Waverley*. He may have still believed in the reality of the clan system, but nobody else did, except, perhaps, for Sir Walter Scott's adoring readers.

Scott's narrative poems made full use of the natural beauty of Scotland, while the *Waverley* novels captured the unique drama of Scottish history. He received a baronetcy from George IV in 1820, soon after his accession, and when the King was persuaded to come to Scotland in 1822 Scott personally stage-managed the royal visit. He thus single-handedly set the scene for the modern come-back of the clan system.

Above,top: *Castle Urquhart passed to the Comyn family soon after it was built in the 13th century. By 1527, after many conflicts, it was in ruins. Before the level of Loch Ness was raised its situation must have been quite spectacular.*

Above: *Inverary Castle, Strathclyde, seat of the Duke of Argyll, the head of Clan Campbell.*

Left: *Clan Donald Centre, Armadale, Skye.*

tradition but not sheepskin grants. With crown confirmation of their own possessions, the Campbells began to turn the feudal screw and demand rents from the MacGregors. Naturally the MacGregor clansmen looked to their own chief and found odious the idea of paying rent to *Mac Chaelein Mor* ('great son of Colin', as the chief of Clan Campbell is always known) or any lesser Campbell.

As more and more MacGregor land was seized, the clansmen became broken men (without blood ties to ensure clan protection) and the MacGregor chief became a mere tenant of Campbell of Glenorchy. To exist at all the MacGregors

Campbell • MacGregor • Colquhoun
MacFarlane • Cameron • Clanranald
Maclean • MacLeod • MacDonald
Mackintosh

The Campbells were numerous,
powerful, and of an ancient lineage
traceable to the first Kings of Argyll.
Charles Campbell of Lochlane (d.1751),
became an advocate, the Scottish
equivalent of a barrister, and this
portrait detail shows a different image
from that usually associated with
Highland clan members.

began to make frequent cattle raids on
Perth and Stirling. They were in a hopeless
position and their impotence was
underlined when the 10th MacGregor
chief attempted to resist Campbell of
Glenorchy's power. He was captured and
beheaded on 7 April 1570 at Balloch
before an audience of invited guests.

By 1603 the Campbells were determined
to finish off the MacGregors. To do so they
displayed a cunning cynicism that was to
characterize the clan at its worst. The Earl
of Argyll, Chief of Clan Campbell,
encouraged a quarrel between the
MacGregors and the Colquhouns of Luss,
Dumbartonshire. A quarrel with
considerable substance – since a
MacGregor raid on Luss territory had
accounted for 300 cows, 100 horses, 400
sheep and 400 goats.

A 300-strong MacGregor force (with
token MacFarlane and Cameron support)
met 700 Colquhouns at Glenfruin on 8
February 1603. An audience of students
and others from Dumbarton and Vale of
Leven had come to watch. Only the most
perverse could have enjoyed the spectacle.
By splitting their force the MacGregors
attacked from two sides and slaughtered

140 Colquhouns for the loss of two
MacGregors. James VI, on the point of
departing for England to unite two
crowns, was furious at this spectacle of
bloodthirsty disunity on his own doorstep.
Before leaving Scotland he had the Privy
Council pass a law outlawing the
MacGregors, abolishing the name
MacGregor, and prohibiting more than
four members of the clan to meet together
at one time.

Any hope the MacGregors may have had
of help from other clans soon dissolved.
Men such as Lochiel, the Cameron chief,
and Clanranald enthusiastically persecuted
the outlawed MacGregors. And of course
Mac Chaelein Mor surpassed himself. Alastair
MacGregor, the 11th chief, surrendered to
the Earl of Argyll in return for a promise
of safe conduct to England where he
intended to plead his clan's case. Argyll
agreed, took MacGregor to Berwick (thus
literally keeping his promise), then brought
him back to Edinburgh for execution.

(Despite their experience of being
outlawed for a total of 139 years – they
had a brief respite after the Restoration –
when the clan was reinstated in 1775, 826
clansmen acknowledged themselves as
MacGregors, thus demonstrating the
remarkable emotional cohesion produced
by the clan principle.)

The clans, then, were anything but
united. They shared customs and a way of
life but were forever each other's worst
enemies. The only time a substantial group
of clans would combine was in support of
the Stuart dynasty (though after the Civil

Right: *The massive Clan Maclean
stronghold of Duart Castle almost rises
out of the cliffs of Duart Bay on the
island of Mull. Its foundations are
13th-century Norman and parts of the
original enclosing wall survive. The
castle has always been the home of the
Macleans with one break, in the
aftermath of Culloden, when Duart
was occupied by the English. In 1910
Sir Fitzroy Maclean repurchased and
restored the castle; it is now lived in
by the present chief, Lord Maclean.*

Below: *The MacGregor Burial
Ground, Central, Trossachs.*

Above: *Dunvegan Castle, Skye, has been the ancestral seat of the MacLeods of MacLeod for over 700 years and still remains their home. Many MacLeod silken relics are on display including the Fairy Flag, which may have been woven in Syria or Rhodes in the 7th century. The Flag has the power to save the MacLeods from destruction on three occasions – to date it has been unfurled twice.*

War there was always the massive exception of Clan Campbell). There was, on the part of the Catholic clans at any rate, a feeling that the Stuart monarch was the Chief of Chiefs. And yet the Stuarts were not conspicuously friendly towards the clans. When they took an interest, it was to make the Highlands conform to Lowland norms.

James VI and I, for example, weary of hearing about blood feuds and disputes, commissioned Lord Ochiltree – assisted by Andrew Knox, Bishop of the Isles – to establish the rule of law in the Isles. Chiefs like Maclean of Duart, Donald Gorm of Sleat, Clanranald, MacLeod and Maclean of Ardgour dined at Duart Castle before being invited aboard Lord Ochiltree's flagship to hear Bishop Knox preach. They got more than a sermon. Once the chiefs were aboard, the ship sailed for Edinburgh where they were imprisoned and only released when they agreed to support Knox in a policy of reforming the Isles.

Thus nine chiefs met at Iona in 1609 and signed the Band and Statutes of Icolmkill, the so-called 'Statutes of Iona'. These measures demanded obedience to the king, ensured Lowland education for the sons of the gentry, abolished firearms and handfasting (a system of trial marriage practised by the clansmen) and called for the discouragement of drinking and bards (presumably on the grounds that the two go together). The idea, of course, was to spread 'civilization' among the clans.

Although the Statutes of Iona did introduce a more legalistic approach to disputes, the traditional way of Highland

strife did not immediately disappear. Shortly after the Statutes had been ratified, for example, Islay was seized by – successively – Sir James MacDonald, then by the Campbells, then by the MacDonalds, then by the Earl of Argyll with a force from London. And as late as 1688, the year of the Glorious Revolution which saw a Stuart king fall and a constitutional monarchy rise to the place of the majestic dogma of divine right, a clan battle was fought in Scotland. This, the battle of Mulroy, the last clan battle of all, took place between the Mackintoshes and the

Achnacarry Castle, the seat of the chiefs of Clan Cameron, has here the present Lord Cameron of Lochiel standing outside it. One of his ancestors was 'The Gentle Lochiel' who pledged his support to Bonnie Prince Charlie in the Jacobite uprising of 1745 thus: 'I'll share the fate of my Prince, and so shall every man over whom nature or fortune hath given me any power.'

MacDonalds of Keppoch. The MacDonalds
held lands in Lochaber (Glen Spean and
Glen Roy) on the clan principle, but the
Mackintosh insisted he had crown
permission – sheepskin grants – to hold
the land. MacDonald scorned such
legalities and, sensing trouble, the
Mackintosh got royal permission to attack
the MacDonalds of Keppoch with an army
of his own clansmen, his allies, and a
company of royal troops under MacKenzie
of Suddie. To meet this force, several sects
of Clan Donald united and annihilated the
Mackintoshes at Mulroy. Because of this
unexpected MacDonald victory and because
of the death of a crown officer, regular
soldiers were sent to destroy the Keppoch
lands and that branch of Clan Donald.

This last of the clan battles was the first
time broadswords were used almost
exclusively by both sides. The government
reaction to it gave the MacDonalds no
alternative but to join Viscount Dundee for
whom they fought superbly at Killiecrankie
for the Stuart cause. When 'Bonnie' Dundee
died at Killiecrankie, the deposed James
foolishly replaced him with a regular
officer whose lack of understanding of the
Highlanders lost him the respect of such
vigorous men as Cameron of Lochiel and

Above: *Eilean Donan Castle, the seat
of Clan MacKenzie, was originally
built in 1220 as part of Alexander II's
defences against the Danes.*

Right, above: *Threave Castle,
Dumfries and Galloway. This 14th-
century Douglas stronghold stands on
an island in the River Dee. In 1455
James II completed his destruction of
the Black Douglases when he bombarded
the castle with 'Mons Meg'.*

Left: *Kilchurn Castle, Strathclyde,
dominates Glen Orchy and was the
original stronghold of the Campbells of
Glenorchy.*

Right: *Drumlanrig Castle, Dumfries
and Galloway, was originally the site
of a 15th-century Douglas stronghold.*

MacDonald of Sleat. Within a few days of his appointment they went home. For his part James lost to William of Orange at the Battle of the Boyne and Britain was set to enter a new constitutional and commercially prosperous era in which there was no place for the clans. That, at least, was William III's point of view.

When he had consolidated his crown in battle, William decided that something drastic would have to be done about the Highlanders who had taken the side of the Stuarts. To Sir John Dalrymple, Master of Stair, Under-Secretary of State for Scotland, the best solution was a scheme to tame the Highlanders. In this he was aided by William and abetted by John Campbell, Earl of Breadalbane. Breadalbane was given £12,000 to buy loyalty from the clan chiefs but, whatever happened to the money (and Breadalbane refused to account for it) there was no appreciable increase in respect for William on the part of the clans.

Accordingly, Stair intimated to Campbell of Breadalbane that 'the Clan Donnel must be rooted out and Lochiel'. On the subject of the money, he added, 'God knows whether the £12,000 sterling had been better employed to settle the Highlands or to ravage them: but since we will make them desperate, I think we should root them out before they can get the help they depend on.'

It was decided that all the clan chiefs should take the oath of allegiance to William not later than 1 January 1692. Those who refused would be met 'by fire and sword and all manner of hostility'. The date was obviously chosen with care, for the harsh Highland winter would partly immobilize the clansmen, a point not lost on Stair. 'The winter time,' he observed, 'is the only season in which we are sure the Highlanders cannot escape, and carry their wives, bairns and cattle to the hills. . . . This is the proper time to maul them in the long dark nights.'

Not surprisingly the clan chiefs took the oath and by 1 January only the powerful MacDonell of Glengarry and old MacIan MacDonald of Glencoe had defaulted. MacIan had tried to make his submission at Fort William on 31 December but, in the absence of a magistrate, was forced to go to Inverary. It was a bad winter and MacIan did not reach Inverary until 2 January. With the sheriff-deputy away, he was unable to take the oath until 6 January. At last William had someone to make an example of, and he wrote to his Highland general: 'If MacIan of Glencoe and that tribe can be well separated from the rest, it will be a proper vindication of public justice to extirpate that sect of thieves.'

So 120 men from the Earl of Argyll's Regiment of Foot, under the command of

Rob Roy, or Red Robert MacGregor, commanded a force of MacGregors in the 1715 rising. He was a brigand whom Sir Walter Scott romanticized: 'he was one of the best swordsmen in the country, partly because his arms were so long that according to tradition he could tie his garters without stooping'. In 1734 he died at Balquhidder as a result of a slight wound sustained in combat with a representative of Clan MacLaren. His statue stands in Stirling.

Captain Robert Campbell of Glenlyon, went to Glencoe to be billeted in the cottages there. The troops were received with the legendary Highland courtesy and for 15 days they shared friendship, food and drink with the Glencoe MacDonalds. Captain Campbell particularly enjoyed playing cards with old MacIan and his sons. Then on 12 February 1692 the Captain received an order from Major Duncanson authorizing the massacre of the MacDonalds of Glencoe. 'You are hereby ordered to fall upon the Rebells, the McDonalds of Glencoe, and putt all to the

Below: *The Pass of Glencoe where, on 13 February 1692,* William of Orange *had the Glencoe MacDonalds massacred by Captain Robert Campbell of Glenlyon. He was promoted to the rank of Colonel.*

Above: *The Atholl Highlanders at Blair Castle are headed by the Duke of Atholl. It is the only private army in Britain and in 1745 Blair was the last private castle in Britain to be besieged.*

Right: *The armoury at Blair Castle. Distinguished visitors to Blair Castle have included Mary, Queen of Scots, Bonnie Prince Charlie and Queen Victoria.*

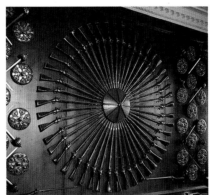

sword under seventy, you are to have a speciall care that the old fox and his sones doe upon no account escape your hands.' The slaughter was to begin at 5 a.m. the following morning.

That evening Captain Campbell played cards with MacIan's sons and said how much he looked forward to dining with the chief the next evening. But as the long dark night of 12 February gave way to the morning of the 13th, the soldiers began their work. MacIan was shot in his bed and his wife had her rings wrenched from her fingers by a soldier's teeth. Then 39 clansmen were attacked in their sleep, bound hand and foot, and murdered in the snow. Their cottages were put on fire as fresh snow began to fall. As the other clansmen realized what was happening they started from their beds and ran towards the caves. Many died in the snow; about half the clan survived. Not only was this a hideous crime, but it was a deliberate mockery of that Highland tradition whereby hospitality was offered even to an enemy.

Highlanders have long memories and even today mention of Glencoe arouses high feeling and bitterness. William of Orange may have demonstrated his power

and determination, but, by contrast, he made the Stuarts look more attractive than they in fact were. When the parliaments of Scotland and England united in 1707 the clans resented their new status as minority groups in 'North Britain' and their hopes were increasingly pinned on the 'king over the water' in France: James Francis Edward, 'the Old Pretender'.

In 1714 George I came to the throne of Great Britain. He was unattractive, poorly equipped intellectually, and largely ignorant of his adopted kingdom. It seemed to the Jacobites the ideal opportunity for the restoration of the Stuarts. However, their rebellion was slow to get under way. The Earl of Mar had been dismissed by the Hanoverian king from his position as Secretary of State for Scotland, and Mar returned to Scotland as leader of the Jacobites. In 1715 he summoned the clan chiefs to a grand hunt at Braemar, raised the Standard for James VIII and III and announced that he, Mar, was Commander-in-Chief, Scotland.

It was a poor appointment because, although Mar had a majority of the Highland chiefs behind him, his military incompetence squandered this potential strength. With around 10,000 clansmen Mar took Perth and then rested on his laurels. In fact he had achieved nothing. At Stirling the Duke of Argyll had only 2,000 men and if Mar had not been intimidated by Argyll's military reputation he could have taken Stirling and pressed on to Edinburgh. As it was Mar did nothing positive. In November he decided to march to Auchterarder but by then Argyll had enlarged his army and was ready to take the Jacobites on. At Sheriffmuir the two sides met. Mar's Highlanders performed magnificently against Argyll's men, but what Mar lacked in tactical expertise Argyll had in abundance. The conflict was indecisive, as the old song all too accurately implies:

> There is some say that we wan,
> And some say that they wan,
> And some say that nan wan at a', man,
> But one thing I'm sure
> That at Sheriffmuir
> A battle there was that I saw, man.

After the battle the Jacobite clans grabbed what booty they could and made off home with it. At the prospect of another battle (and therefore more booty) with Argyll the clans rallied again early in 1716. Mar, however, settled for retreat and, tired of their leader's procrastination, the clans deserted. James Francis Edward had the same idea. A month after landing at Peterhead he had seen enough and left Scotland for France with Mar. After the collapse of the rebellion the Highlanders were left to take the consequences. Punitive measures really began after

Left: Glen Shiel, associated with the MacKenzies and the MacGregors.

Left, below: Dunrobin Castle, Highland, was the ancestral seat of the Dukes and Earls of Sutherland and built originally in the late 13th century. The present baronial residence was designed in 1835–50 by Sir Charles Barry, architect of the Houses of Parliament.

Below: Wade's Bridge, Aberfeldy. Sent to pacify the Highlands, General Wade built between 1726 and 1737 a network of roads and bridges totalling 260 miles. By opening up the Highlands they gave the Government more control over the troublesome clans. This particular bridge in Aberfeldy was built in 1733.

another Stuart adventure in 1719 when a planned Scottish diversion fizzled out at the pass of Glenshiel.

It was obvious to the government that as long as the Highlands were impenetrable the clans would have the military advantage in any recrudescence of Jacobitism. General George Wade, Scotland's Commander-in-Chief, opened up the Highlands with a network of roads. Under the Disarming Act Wade deprived the clans of many weapons. Finally, he reorganized the six Highland Independent Companies and required them to police the Highlands.

In 1724 General Wade estimated that there were around 22,000 men capable of bearing arms – of whom more than half would be likely to support a Stuart rebellion. From these figures we can project a total Highland population of around 150,000 at that time. Therefore what the government feared was not the quantity of the opposition, but the quality of fighting the clansmen were capable of. Most feared of all was the Highland charge. This was a pre-emptive strike that

The Macnab (1734–1816) by Raeburn. Francis Macnab, 16th Chief of Macnab, resplendent in his uniform as Lieutenant-Colonel of the Royal Breadalbane Volunteers. He never married, although he is said to have courted a lady in vain and 'told her as an irresistible charm that he had the most beautiful burying-ground in the world' – on the island of Inchbuie. Of his 32 children none was legitimate.

depended on sheer recklessness to terrorize the enemy. Advancing three deep the Highlanders would break into small units led by chieftains. With a targe on their left arm, a dirk in their left fist, they rushed forward firing pistols – if they had any – then drew their broadswords and slashed into the enemy. This technique was to become feared during the '45 Uprising. It was to be, in fact, Bonnie Prince Charlie's secret weapon.

Thirty years after his father's failure in the '15 Charles Edward Louis Philip Casimir Stuart landed at Eriskay – a tiny Hebridean island – with seven followers and no armed support. He had come to a country he knew nothing of to take a crown he had never seen. As Scott put it in Waverley, Bonnie Prince Charlie 'threw himself upon the mercy of his countrymen, rather like a hero of romance than a calculating politician'. When MacDonald of Boisdale told him to go home Charles said,

'I am come home'. He then predicted that 'my faithful Highlanders will stand by me'.

With naïve confidence in the justice of his cause Charles won the astute Cameron of Lochiel to his side and on 19 August 1745 raised his Standard at Glenfinnan before some 1,200 clansmen. From Glenfinnan he went from strength to strength, first taking Edinburgh and then spectacularly defeating Sir John Cope at Prestonpans. Bonnie Prince Charlie was in command of all Scotland. That was not, however, enough for a Stuart.

With his 5,000-strong Highland army he marched into England taking Carlisle, Preston, Lancaster, Manchester, Macclesfield and then Derby. Suddenly,

Below, left: *Glenfinnan. Here at the head of Loch Shiel, Charles raised the Standard of the House of Stuart on 19 August 1745. The column was erected in 1815 by a descendant of a devoted Jacobite.*

Right: *Duncan Forbes, 10th Laird of Culloden, erected the Culloden Memorial Cairn in 1881. The Cairn marks the most fiercely contested part of the battlefield; a service is held here annually in memory of the struggle.*

Bottom right: *The Black Watch Monument at Aberfeldy pays tribute to the military police force set up by George Wade, with men from six companies commanded by Lord Lovat, Grant of Ballindalloch, Munro of Culcairn and three Campbells.*

Below, right: *Drummond Castle, Tayside, the beautiful medieval mansion in which lives the Drummond Chief, the Earl of Perth.*

when within 150 miles of London, the Prince's advisers began to panic realizing they faced an army some six times larger than their own. The Prince wanted to go on. He had known only victory so far and reasoned that he had an excellent chance of success. Caution, however, prevailed. Although he said: 'Rather than go back, I would wish to be twenty feet under ground', Charles was persuaded to retreat. And retreat the Highland army did, as far as Inverness. At Culloden, on 16 April 1746, an exhausted, starving, ill-equipped Highland army was attacked by 9,000 regular troops under the command of the Duke of Cumberland who had never won a battle before.

It took Cumberland only 25 minutes to destroy the Highland army. He could hardly have failed: the Highlanders had rations of one biscuit apiece and had just taken part in a disorganized night march. They were in no condition to do battle. Cumberland, the 'Butcher', showed no mercy. The wounded were left to die, the captured were burned alive and mutilated and the dead were left to rot, while villages and towns Cumberland felt were sympathetic to Jacobitism were destroyed. The Prince escaped, became a fugitive in the Hebrides, then returned to Europe to embark on a pathetic life of debauchery. The Highlanders were crushed. Their spirit was finally broken with a new Disarming Act, a ban on Highland dress, and a planned campaign to discourage the Gaelic tongue and make the clansmen God-fearing

Protestant folk. So successful was this campaign that by 1782 the government could lift the ban on Highland dress.

It may seem strange that Lowland Scotland could rejoice over the extermination of the Highland way of life, but it did. Scotland was two nations – one commercially minded in motivation and English in sympathy, the other agricultural and Gaelic in temperament. And yet no sooner was the English-speaking world rid of the clans than it wanted to preserve their memory. It wanted the picturesque costumes without the Gaelic-speaking barbarian inside them. More than anyone else, Sir Walter Scott romanticized the clans and once the movement had begun it became a craze. For example, in 1800 the firm of William Wilson & Son of Bannockburn manufactured very few tartans. By the time of George IV's visit to Edinburgh they manufactured 150. Today there are hundreds of tartans, with commercial variations being added to them all the time.

George IV's visit in 1822 was the apotheosis of the Highland craze initiated by Scott. Indeed Scott was involved in the arrangements and personally stage-managed the visit. George appeared in kilt and plaid in, naturally, the Stuart tartan. After a dinner in Parliament House, George proposed a toast – 'Health to the chieftains and clans, and God Almighty bless the Land of Cakes. Drink this with three times

three, gentlemen.' He also flattered Lady Anne Grant by telling her she was 'truly an object fit to raise the chivalry of a clan'.

It was only left to Victoria and Albert to make a museum out of their Scotophilia. After holidaying with Victoria at Balmoral, Prince Albert bought the estate, demolished the old castle, and commissioned a grandiose new castle which he personally supervised – right down to the tartan carpets. Victoria called Balmoral her 'dear paradise' and could never exhaust its charms or the historical associations of the Highlands. After visiting the Glenfinnan monument in 1873 the Queen wrote in her diary: 'What a scene it must have been in 1745! And here was I, the descendant of the Stuarts and of the very king whom Prince Charles sought to overthrow, sitting and walking about quite privately and peaceably.'

Above: *Clan gatherings are a popular feature of Scottish summer life, and in this one a pipe band is marching in Stirlingshire. Other pictures on these pages show a tiny sample of the various types of clan memorials all over Scotland.*

Below: *The Clan Gunn Museum at Caithness.*

Below, left: *The memorial to the Clan Macrae at Dunblane.*

Above: Highland Games at Callander. These games recall traditional clan meetings and are an example of the deep affection Scotsmen feel for that part of their history that was extinguished.

Above right: Balmoral Castle, Grampian, Queen Victoria's 'dear paradise'. Originally Robert II had a hunting lodge here, then Sir Malcolm Drummond built a tower. The Gordon Earls of Huntly bought the estate in the 15th century.

Right: A Highland Gathering at Braemar.

Below: A fine cross carved c.1470, at Kilmory Chapel. The Latin inscription reads 'This is the cross of Alexander Macmillan'.

It was true. The clans had been tamed out of existence and only survived in the memory. Yet it is a powerful memory that makes everyone with Scottish connections long to be affiliated to a clan. A powerful memory that makes the clansmen such an object of adoration all over the English-speaking world. Today there are almost a thousand pipe bands in Scotland, the Scots Ancestry Research Council handles more than a thousand genealogical enquiries a year for Americans alone, and there are more than a thousand tartans (though most of them would have baffled the clansmen). Clan societies preserve old castles, international clan-gatherings are held, and all the time the motor-car noses its way into the straths and glens looking for evidence that the clans really were

what we believe they were.

Now the clans only exist in the dimension of history. At the time of their defeat they were an anachronism in terms of Lowland economic and social organization. But they had a language and a culture and a landscape of their own. And they were taken from them. Perhaps the reason that people feel so sentimental towards the clans is that their exit from history was so dramatically total, so tragically sudden. It is a mood perhaps best expressed in that exile's lament, 'The Canadian Boat Song':

From the lone shieling and the distant island
   Mountains divide us and a waste of seas;
But still the blood is strong, the heart is Highland
   And we in dreams behold the Hebrides.

SOME CLANS AND SEPTS AND THEIR TARTANS

A clan is a collection of families supposed to have a common ancestor and subject to a single chieftain. They usually bear the same surname.
A sept is a division of a clan.
The tartans are in italic.

Abbot, *Macnab*
Adam, *Gordon*
Adamson, *Mackintosh*
Alexander, *MacAlister or MacDonell of Glengarry*
Allan, *MacDonald of Clanranald or MacFarlane*
Allison, *Allison*
Anderson, *Anderson and Ross*
Andrew, *Ross*
Angus, *Angus and MacInnes*
Armstrong, *Armstrong*
Arthur, *MacArthur, Campbell or MacDonald*
Baillie, *Baillie*
Bain, *Bayne, MacBean, MacKay or Macnab*
Baird, *Baird*
Barclay, *Barclay*
Barrie, *Dunbar, Farquharson or Gordon*
Bartholomew, *Leslie or MacFarlane*
Baxter, *Baxter and Macmillan*
Bell, *Macmillan*
Berkeley, *Barclay*
Black, *Lamont, MacGregor or Maclean*
Boyd, *Boyd and Stewart*
Brewer, *Drummond or MacGregor*
Brodie, *Brodie*
Brown, *Lamont or Macmillan*
Bruce, *Brus, Bruce*
Buchan, *Buchan (Cumming)*
Buchanan, *Buchanan*
Burnett, *Burnett and Campbell*
Burns, *Burns and Campbell*
Cairns, *Ferguson or Grant*
Calder, *Campbell of Cawdor*
Cameron, *Cameron*
Campbell, *Campbell, and Argyll, Breadalbane, Cawdor or Loudoun*
Carmichael, *Carmichael, and MacDougall, Stewart of Appin or Stewart of Galloway*
Carnegie, *Carnegie*
Chalmers, *Cameron*
Chisholm, *Chisholm*
Christie, *Christie or Farquharson*
Clark, *Clarkson, Clerk, Clark and Cameron, or Clan Chattan*
Cochrane, *Cochrane and MacDonald*
Cockburn, *Cockburn*
Collier, *Robertson*
Colman, *Buchanan*
Colquhoun, *Colquhoun*
Cook, *Stewart*
Coulson, *MacDonald*
Cowan, *Colquhoun or MacDougall*
Crawford, *Crawford and Lindsay*
Cumming, *Cumming*
Cunningham, *Cunningham*
Currie, *MacDonald or Macpherson*
Dalziel, *Dalzell*
Davidson, *Davie, Davis, Davison, Dawson, Davidson*
Dewar, *Macnab or Menzies*
Donald, *Donaldson, Macdonald*
Douglas, *Douglas*

Dove, *Buchanan*
Dow, *Buchanan or Davidson*
Drummond, *Drummond*
Duff, *MacDuff*
Duffie, *Duffy, Macfie*
Dunbar, *Dunbar*
Duncan, *Duncan and Robertson*
Dundas, *Dundas*
Elder, *Mackintosh*
Elliot, *Elliot*
Erskine, *Erskine*
Ewan, *Ewen, Ewing, MacLachlan*
Farquhar, *Farquharson*
Ferguson, *Fergusson*
Findlay, *Finlay, Farquharson*
Fleming, *Murray*
Fletcher, *Fletcher and MacGregor*
Forbes, *Forbes*
Forsyth, *Forsyth*
France, *Stewart*
Fraser, *Frazer, Fraser*
Fullarton, *Fullerton, Stuart of Bute*
Galbraith, *Galbraith and MacDonald, or MacFarlane*
Georgeson, *Gunn*
Gibb, *Gibson, Buchanan*
Gilbert, *Gilbertson, Buchanan*
Gilchrist, *MacLachlan or Ogilvy*
Gillespie, *Macpherson*
Gilmore, *Morrison*
Gilroy, *Grant or MacGillivray*
Glen, *Glennie, Mackintosh*
Gordon, *Gordon*
Graeme, *Graham, Graham (Menteith or Montrose)*
Grant, *Grant*
Gray, *Stewart of Atholl or Sutherland*
Gregor(y), *Greig, MacGregor*
Grier, *Grierson, MacGregor*
Gunn, *Gunn*
Hamilton, *Hamilton*
Hardie, *Hardy, Farquharson or Mackintosh*
Harper, *Buchanan*
Hawes, *Campbell*
Hawthorn, *MacDonald*
Hay, *Hay*
Henderson, *Henderson and Gunn, or MacDonald*
Home, *Hume, Home*
Houston, *MacDonald*
Hunter, *Hunter*
Huntly, *Huntly and Gordon*
Hutcheson, *Hutchinson, MacDonald*
Inglis, *Inglis*
Innes, *Innes*
Irvine, *Irvine*
Jameson, *Jamieson, Gunn or Stuart of Bute*
Johnson, *Gunn or MacDonald*
Johnston(e), *Johnstone*
Kay, *Davidson*
Kean, *Keene, Gunn or MacDonald*
Keith, *Keith and Macpherson, or Sutherland*
Kellie, *Kelly, MacDonald*
Kendrick, *MacNaughton*
Kennedy, *Kennedy and Cameron*
Kenneth, *MacKenzie*
Kerr, *Kerr*
Kilpatrick, *Colquhoun*
King, *Colquhoun or MacGregor*
Lamb, *Lamont*
Lang, *Leslie or MacDonald*
Laurence, *Law, MacLaren*
Lennox, *Lennox and MacFarlane, or Stewart*
Leslie, *Leslie*
Lewis, *MacLeod of Lewis*

Lindsay, *Lindsay*
Livingstone, *Livingstone, and Stewart of Appin or MacDougall*
Logan, *Logan or MacLennan*
Love, *Mackinnon*
Low, *MacLaren*
Lucas, *Luke, Lamont*
Lumsden, *Lumsden and Forbes*
Lyall, *Sinclair*
Lyon, *Farquharson or Lamont*
MacAdam, *MacGregor*
MacAllister, *MacAllister*
MacAlpine, *MacAlpine*
MacArthur, *MacArthur*
MacAulay, *MacAulay and MacLeod of Lewis*
MacBride, *MacDonald*
MacCall, *MacDonald*
MacCallum, *MacCallum and Malcolm*
MacConnell, *MacDonald*
MacCormack, *MacCormick, Buchanan or MacLaine of Lochbuie*
MacCulloch, *MacDougall, Munro or Ross*
MacDonald, *MacDonald and associated septs*
MacDonell, *MacDonald and MacDonell of Glengarry or of Keppoch*
MacDougall, *MacDougall*
MacDowell, *MacDougall*
MacDuff, *MacDuff*
MacEwan, *MacEwen, MacEwen and MacLachlan*
MacFarlane, *MacFarlane*
Macfee, *Macfie, Macfie*
MacGill, *MacGill*
MacGillivray, *MacGillivray*
MacGowan, *MacGowan, MacDonald or Macpherson*
MacGregor, *MacGregor*
MacGuire, *Macquarrie*
MacHugh, *MacDonald*
Macintyre, *Macintyre*
Mackay, *Mackay*
MacKenzie, *MacKenzie*
Mackie, *Mackay*
Mackinlay, *Mackinley, Mackinlay and Buchanan, or Farquharson or MacFarlane or Stewart of Appin*
Mackinnon, *Mackinnon*
Mackintosh, *Mackintosh*
MacLachlan, *MacLachlan*
MacLaren, *MacLaren*
Maclean, *Maclean of Duart*
MacLellan, *MacLellan and MacDonald*
MacLennan, *Logan or MacLennan tartan*
MacLeod, *MacLeod (Harris or Lewis)*
Macmillan, *Macmillan*
Macnab, *Macnab*
MacNaughton, *MacNaughton*
MacNeil(l), *MacNeil(l)*
MacPhail, *MacPhail and Cameron, Mackay or Clan Chattan*
Macpherson, *Macpherson*
Macquarrie, *Macquarrie*
MacQueen, *MacQueen and MacDonald*
Macrae, *Macrae*
Malcolm, *Malcolm*
Mann, *Manson, Gunn*
Marr, *Mar*
Marshall, *Keith, Marshall and Austin tartan*
Martin, *Cameron or MacDonald*
Matheson, *Matheson*
Maxwell, *Maxwell*
May, *MacDonald*
Melville, *Melville*
Melvin, *MacBeth*
Menzies, *Menzies*

Middleton, *Middleton or Innes*
Mill, *Milne, Gordon, Innes or Ogilvy*
Millar, *Miller, MacFarlane*
Mitchell, *Mitchell or Innes*
Monro, *Monroe, Munro*
Montgomerie, *Montgomerie*
More, *Leslie*
Morgan, *Morgan and Mackay*
Morrison, *Morrison*
Morton, *Douglas*
Muir, *Muir*
Munro, *Monroe, Munro*
Murdoch, *MacDonald or Macpherson*
Murphy, *MacDonald*
Murray, *Murray (Atholl or Tullibardine)*
Napier, *Napier and MacFarlane*
Neal, *Neil (l), MacNeil*
Neilson, *MacKay or MacNeil (l)*
Nelson, *Gunn*
Nicol, *Nicolson, Nicolson (MacNicol) and MacLeod of Lewis*
Nisbet, *Nisbet*
Noble, *Mackintosh*
Norman, *MacLeod of Harris or Sutherland*
Ogilvie, *Ogilvy, Ogilvy*
Paterson, *MacLaren*
Patrick, *Lamont*
Paul, *Cameron, MacKay or Mackintosh*
Peter, *Petrie, MacGregor*
Rae, *Macrae*
Ramsay, *Ramsay*
Rankin, *Rankin and MacLean of Duart*
Reid, *Robertson*
Ritchie, *Mackintosh*
Robb, *MacFarlane or Robertson*
Robertson, *Robertson*
Robson, *Gunn*
Rose, *Rose*
Ross, *Ross*
Roy, *Robertson*
Russell, *Russell and Cumming*
Sanderson, *MacDonell of Glengarry*
Scott, *Scott*
Seaton, *Seton, Seton*
Shannon, *MacDonald*
Shaw, *Shaw and Mackintosh*
Sim, *Sime, Simon, Simpson, Fraser*
Sinclair, *Sinclair*
Small, *Murray*
Smith, *Clan Chattan, Gow, Smith*
Spence, *MacDuff*
Stark, *Robertson*
Stewart, *Stewart (Appin, Atholl, Galloway, Royal, etc)*
Stuart of Bute, *Stuart of Bute*
Sutherland, *Sutherland*
Swan, *Macqueen*
Taylor, *Taylor and Cameron*
Thomas, *Thompson, Campbell, MacTavish or MacThomas*
Todd, *Gordon*
Turner, *Lamont*
Urquhart, *Urquhart*
Wallace, *Wallis, Wallace*
Walters, *Forbes*
Watson, *Buchanan or Watson*
Watt, *Buchanan*
Weir, *Weir and MacFarlane, or MacNaughton*
White, *Lamont, MacGregor*
Wilkinson, *MacDonald*
Williamson, *Gunn or Mackay*
Wilson, *Wilson and Gunn or Innes*
Wright, *Macintyre*
Wylie, *Gunn or MacFarlane*